D1301382

Máquinas maravillosas/Mighty Machines
Barcos de rescate/Rescue Boats

por/by Carol K. Lindeen

Traducción/Translation: Martín Luis Guzmán Ferrer, Ph.D.
Editor Consultor/Consulting Editor: Dra. Gail Saunders-Smith

Capstone
press

Mankato, Minnesota

Please return to:
ONEONTA PUBLIC LIBRARY
221 2nd Street S.
Oneonta, AL 35121
205-274-7641

Pebble Plus is published by Capstone Press,
151 Good Counsel Drive, P.O. Box 669, Mankato, Minnesota 56002.
www.capstonepress.com

Copyright © 2006 by Capstone Press. All rights reserved.
No part of this publication may be reproduced in whole or in part, or stored in a retrieval
system, or transmitted in any form or by any means, electronic, mechanical,
photocopying, recording, or otherwise, without written permission of the publisher.
For information regarding permission, write to Capstone Press,
151 Good Counsel Drive, P.O. Box 669, Dept. R, Mankato, Minnesota 56002.
Printed in the United States of America

1 2 3 4 5 6 11 10 09 08 07 06

Library of Congress Cataloging-in-Publication Data
Lindeen, Carol K., 1976–
[Rescue boats. Spanish & English]
Barcos de rescate/de Carol K. Lindeen = Rescue boats/by Carol K. Lindeen.
p. cm.—(Pebble plus. Máquinas maravillosas=Pebble plus. Mighty machines)
Includes index.
ISBN-13: 978-0-7368-5876-2 (hardcover)
ISBN-10: 0-7368-5876-8 (hardcover)
1. Search and rescue boats—Juvenile literature. I. Title. II. Series: Pebble plus. Máquinas maravillosas.
VM466.S4L5518 2005
623.826—dc22   2005019058

Summary: Simple text and photographs present rescue boats, their parts, and how people use rescue boats.

Editorial Credits
Martha E. H. Rustad, editor; Jenny Marks, bilingual editor; Eida del Risco, Spanish copy editor; Molly Nei,
   set designer; Kate Opseth and Ted Williams, book designers; Jo Miller, photo researcher; Scott Thoms,
   photo editor

Photo Credits
Check Six 2004/Barry Smith, 1, 17
Corbis/Cordaiy Photo Library Ltd./John Framar, 6–7; James Marshall, 18–19; Neil Rebinowitz, 21
Corbis Saba/Najlah Feanny, 13
DVIC/PHC Gloria Montgomery, 5; SSGT Michael Buytas, 14–15
Photo Network/Mary Messenger, 10–11
Unicorn Stock Photos/Dede Gilman, 9
U.S. Coast Guard Photo/PA3 Anthony Juarez, cover

Note to Parents and Teachers

The Mighty Machines set supports national standards related to science, technology, and society. This book describes and illustrates rescue boats. The images support early readers in understanding the text. The repetition of words and phrases helps early readers learn new words. This book also introduces early readers to subject-specific vocabulary words, which are defined in the Glossary section. Early readers may need assistance to read some words and to use the Table of Contents, Glossary, Internet Sites, and Index sections of the book.

Table of Contents

Tabla de contenidos

What Are Rescue Boats?

Rescue boats help people

in danger on oceans,

big lakes, and rivers.

¿Qué son los barcos de rescate?

Los barcos de rescate ayudan

a las personas en los océanos,

los grandes lagos y los ríos.

Parts and Gear

Rescue boats have antennas.
Antennas help rescue crews
find boats in trouble.

Las partes y el equipo

Los barcos de rescate tienen antenas.
Las antenas ayudan a la tripulación
de rescate a encontrar los barcos que
están en peligro.

antennas/antenas

Rescue boats have
strong ropes. The crew
uses ropes to tow boats
to safety.

Los barcos de rescate tienen
unas cuerdas muy fuertes. La tripulación
usa las cuerdas para remolcar
a los barcos y ponerlos a salvo.

rope/cuerda

Rescue workers wear
life jackets to stay safe.
Rescue boats have extra
life jackets for the people
they rescue.

Los trabajadores de los barcos de
rescate usan chalecos salvavidas que
los protegen del peligro. Los barcos de
rescate llevan más chalecos salvavidas
para las personas que van a rescatar.

To the Rescue

A rescue boat gets a call.

Another boat is broken

and is sinking.

Al rescate

Un barco de rescate recibe

una llamada. Otro barco

se ha roto y se está hundiendo.

13

The crew rushes

onto the rescue boat.

They get ready

for the rescue.

La tripulación corre

al barco de rescate.

Ellos se preparan

para el rescate.

A crew member steers
the rescue boat.
The rescue boat speeds
over big waves.

Un miembro de la tripulación
timonea el barco de rescate.
El barco de rescate navega
veloz sobre las olas.

TILLAMOOK
BAY

30619

The rescue crew finds the
people who need help.
The rescue boat carries
everyone safely to shore.

La tripulación encuentra
a las personas que necesitan ayuda.
El barco de rescate las conduce
a salvo a la orilla.

Rescue crews use
rescue boats to help people
in emergencies.

La tripulación de un barco de
rescate usa el barco para ayudar
a las personas en una emergencia.

Glossary

antenna—a tall wire that receives radio signals

crew—a group of people who work together

emergency—a sudden and dangerous situation; people need to deal with emergencies quickly.

life jacket—a vest that floats; people wear life jackets to stay safe in boats and in water; life jackets help people float in water.

steer—to make a boat or car go in a certain direction

tow—to pull along behind; a rescue boat can tow another boat that is broken or damaged.

Glosario

antena—alambre elevado que recibe señales
de radio

chaleco salvavidas—chaleco que flota;
las personas usan chalecos salvavidas para
su seguridad en los barcos y en el agua;
los chalecos salvavidas ayudan a las personas
a flotar en el agua.

emergencia—situación inesperada y peligrosa;
las personas tienen que actuar rápidamente en
las emergencias.

remolcar—jalar una cosa desde atrás; un barco
de rescate puede remolcar a un barco roto
o estropeado.

timonear—hacer que un barco vaya en
cierta dirección

tripulación—grupo de personas que trabaja
en equipo en un barco o avión

Internet Sites

FactHound offers a safe, fun way to find Internet sites related to this book. All of the sites on FactHound have been researched by our staff.

Here's how:

1) Visit *www.facthound.com*

2) Type in this special code **0736836551** for age-appropriate sites. Or enter a search word related to this book for a more general search.

3) Click on the **FETCH IT** button.

FactHound will fetch the best sites for you!

Sitios de Internet

FactHound te ofrece una manera segura y divertida para encontrar sitios de Internet relacionados con este libro. Todos los sitios de FactHound han sido investigados por nuestro equipo. Es posible que los sitios no estén en español.

Así:

1) Ve a *www.facthound.com*

2) Teclea la clave especial **0736836551** para los sitios apropiados por edad. O teclea una palabra relacionada con este libro para una búsqueda más general.

3) Clic en el botón de **FETCH IT**.

¡FactHound buscará los mejores sitios para ti!

Index

Índice